WHERE WOMEN CREATE™

BOOK OF ORGANIZATION:

WHERE WOMEN CREATE™

BOOK OF ORGANIZATION:

The Art of Creating Order

BY: JO PACKHAM & THE PUBLISHERS OF SOMERSET STUDIO

WWC
PRESS

EDITOR
Michelle Hainer

PRODUCTION MANAGER
Brandy Shay

ART DIRECTOR
Matt Shay

AMANDA CRAMES

WWC·PRESS
An Imprint of Sterling Publishing
387 Park Avenue South
New York, NY 10016

WWC Press and the distinctive WWC Press logo are registered trademarks of Jo Packham

ISBN 978-1-4027-9151-2

Distributed in Canada by Sterling Publishing
c/o Canadian Manda Group, 165 Dufferin Street
Toronto, Ontario, Canada M6K 3H6
Distributed in the United Kingdom by GMC Distribution Services
Castle Place, 166 High Street, Lewes, East Sussex, England BN7 1XU
Distributed in Australia by Capricorn Link (Australia) Pty. Ltd.
P.O. Box 704, Windsor, NSW 2756, Australia

For information about custom editions, special sales, and premium and corporate purchases, please contact Sterling Special Sales at 800-805-5489 or specialsales@sterlingpublishing.com.

Manufactured in the United States of America

2 4 6 8 10 9 7 5 3 1

www.sterlingpublishing.com

It is such an honor to be authoring books for Sterling Publishing under my very own imprint: WWC PRESS. *Book of Organization* will be the first title to be published under this imprint … I am sincerely both humbled and proud.

Because my first book for WWC PRESS is on the "ART of Creating Order" I decided that, for the first time in longer than I can remember, I should dedicate the time to make certain that my creative space was both orderly and arty. How can I author a book such as this if I, my studio, was not?!

I came to the studio early one Saturday morning and decided that I MUST be organized. Where do I start? What organizational system do I use? What do I keep and what do I let go of? As I moved from chair to chair I decided to completely reorganize —differently than before and definitely more thoroughly. Everything must be in order, not only on the surface so that it looks beautiful but also inside the boxes and the drawers and the oversized hutches so that I really know what I have that I remember … and what I have forgotten.

It always fascinates me how completely unaware we are of how much we emulate our parents. Her entire life, my mom lived on very little, so from an early age she was forced to be practical and I think because of this she was the very definition of organized. She had to be; everything had to have a purpose, had to be utilized on so many different levels, and had to be well taken care of so that it would last a very long time. All of her nice things were always wrapped in clean white tissue, placed in perfectly sized boxes, and stacked neatly in her drawer. Her few tiny collections were hidden in secret containers in her cupboards. Those items needed in her everyday life were always well cared for, in plain sight, and arranged for easy use.

My dad, on the other hand, was all about the show. Everything he did he did with such style. My mom would often say, "Your dad has a champagne appetite but a beer budget," but for him it didn't matter. My dad knew how to make a statement regardless if he had a dollar or a hundred dollars in his pocket.

So this, my first book under my new imprint, is dedicated to the two of them. They taught me everything I know, made me believe there wasn't anything I could not do, and helped me to understand how all of it can be done the way it should be: organized with a style that can only be referred to as "ART"!

I Love You Mom & Dad

I Miss You

Me

BATHROOMS
BATHROOMS
BEDROOMS
BEDROOMS
BLACK & WHITE
CLASSIC
COASTAL
CONTEMPORARY
COUNTRY
DESIGNER SPOTLIGHT
DINING ROOMS
DOORS & WINDOWS
EARLY CALIFORNIA
EXTERIOR
FF&E
FINISHES
FIREPLACES
GALLERY/DISPLAY
HOLIDAY DECOR
RESTAURANTS & BARS
RUSTIC
SOURCES
SOUTHWEST
SPECIALTY ROOMS
STAIRCASES
TRADITIONAL
URBAN
UTILITY ROOMS
WINDOW TREATMENTS

CONTENTS

THE SYSTEM

The System—The ART of Creating Order: the studios, the creators who own them, and their notes on "organizing" are here to inspire more than to educate.

For all of us featured on these pages, creating order is a system that is more about what works for each creative soul individually rather than what the "experts" profess as the right or wrong way to organize anyone and everyone's creative space. On these pages, there are few written words because we believe that when you begin to create your system to organize your space, "one picture is worth more than a thousand words"!

THE ROOM

When gathering bottles to store your collections sometimes "diversity" is more interesting than repetition ... and sometimes not!

THE ROOM: size is the least important consideration in regards to your creative space. You can create whatever you can imagine regardless of where you are.

For some, small spaces are the better choice. It is here that you feel "surrounded and secure." In a smaller space all of your equipment and supplies, as well as your thoughts and your visions, must be well organized and easily within your reach. And this is your private space with only room for you and your ideas and your conviction of what is possible.

For some, the more space, the more inspired you become. It is here that you have a "stage" all of your own on which to bring your art to life. Here in these bigger spaces there are no boundaries or borders ... only the freedom to search, to study, to practice, and to present in whatever materials, technique, or style that is your choice of the day.

In a larger space, you also have the luxury of working on your art, leaving it before it is complete, and returning another day to analyze and redesign. Here, there is room to share a worktable, a bookshelf, a desk, or a new idea with your children, your husband, your closest friend, or a student who wants to learn all that you can teach them. It is here that there is room for "everything" that you ever imagined or believed that you would create ... as soon as you had a "larger" space that you could honestly call your own!

In your room, today, any piece of furniture can be anything you want it to be and tomorrow it can be something else entirely. This vintage shoe rack is over 100 years old and with new glass shelves it holds jars and jars of beads ... today.

No space must be left empty and unused ... every space is perfect sometime for something!

Your most important memories must NOT be stuffed inside of a box, neatly folded in a drawer, tucked away on a closest shelf, or carefully positioned permanently on the pages of an album. Those greeting cards, artist's prints, pieces of fabric, baby clothes, exotic department store sacks, jewelry, and handmade collectables that are most dear to you should be put on a the wall that you see everyday. It is then that you can enjoy the moment and the memories spontaneously and without forethought or follow-through.

Absolutely every piece of furniture that finds a home in your studio should either be a memory or be useful ... there simply isn't room for anything else! And each piece must always be a thoughtfully planned and executed segment of the "whole."

Nothing should ever be ordinary!

The shelves pictured below were made from broken pieces of discarded vintage stair balusters, newly purchased raw wood railings, and shelves that were cut from pressed board. They are all that you need and want: eclectic, imaginative, and functional.

Create individual spaces in your room so that each is as recognizable as you are. Each tiny division in this creative world you have built is important, for they give you "your" space for whatever it is that you want to do at any particular moment.

Paint one small corner your favorite shade of aqua or taupe or peach so you can sit quietly and write on the pages of your journal. And then paint one area as if it were a sunset burning in the early evening sky because it is here where you will always be inspired and strive to be great.

These spaces hold and display your most treasured pieces. They keep your collection of magazines in stacks or on shelves so they are ready for the ritual of the tearing-out of the pages. Here there are drawers that are filled with papers, pieces of jewelry, some things vintage and some things new, but all things needed when you are ready to work.

Do not neglect any part of your creative space. Each is as important as the other and all must be treated with unquestionable gratitude as if each were the only space that you could truly call your own.

THE CABINET

It is important for me that all of the drawers in my cabinets have labels on them, and that the labels are distinctly different for each set of drawers, that they are easy to read, and that each could be considered a "piece of art" in and of itself. If a drawer is closed and there is no label, it is as if the drawer were empty and its contents disappeared.

The difficulties in labeling seem to be:

1. In what to make the label out of. If it is paper, you must be careful that the paper is heavy enough not to tear and that this paper label is attached in a place on the drawer front where it will not get dirty when the drawer is opened.

2. In how to attach the labels to the drawer fronts so they are permanent enough to stay until you want to change them, but then removable without damaging the front of the drawer. Depending on what the label is made of, and how the surface of the drawer is finished, you can use a glue gun, double stick tape, glue dots, or scrapbook adhesive strips.

Also important is that each of the drawers has some kind of dividers, compartments, or containers that fit "perfectly" inside of the drawer. Every organized creative space must be as beautifully and well organized in the places that cannot be seen as it is in those places that are obvious to a discerning eye.

THE SHELF

I think that I can honestly say that collectors and those of us who work with our hands LOVE our shelves ... they are such an essential component to our decorating and organizing. And the truly lovely thing about shelves is that they come in all shapes and sizes, they can be free standing, hung, or placed at the back of a desk against a wall. When filled with all of the things that we must not only display but use, they are pieces of art that capture our imagination!

Vintage linens

Vintage lace

Vintage ribbon

Vintage ribbon

BIG BOWL of LOVE

ITE FOR LIFE

NOËL RILEY FITCH

A WEBLIN'S CHEESE ESSENTIALS

ARTISAN CHEESE MAKING AT HOME

Did You Kn

what the

Finished Product

een Market BAKING BOOK

at home Cook Your Way to the Good Life

THE CONTAINER

Some of my most "collectable pieces" are the containers I use to organize all of my "everything"! I love glass containers most, bottles really, because I can see what is inside. If the container hides its contents, then it must have a label or the contents are quickly forgotten.

On my shelves I organize my clear jars first by "content color" and then by "content". I can see inside so my passion for "organized color" dictates which jar goes on which shelf right next to what.

I am often so mesmerized by containers that I forget that when buying anything to help organize my creative space, I need to be careful to first buy those that have wide openings. Wide openings are essential so that I can easily get the beads or sewing bobbins or paintbrushes both in to and out of the bottle. Jars or bottles or boxes with small openings are limited in what can be stored inside of them.

And I often remind myself that those containers that are perfectly round or with squared sides are preferable. Uneven sides or unusually shaped bottles are difficult to display on shelves or arrange neatly inside of drawers. And the color of a container only matters if its contents need to be remembered or selected by its colors. Glitter, beads, buttons are all more efficiently stored in clear glass containers so that you can easily see what it is you have and what color it is.

Use containers for "all" things in many ways ... these are actually wooden drawer organizers for the kitchen that neatly and securely stack on top of one another and hold my collection of Japanese "funky junk."

My Collections: because my life is overflowing with too much of almost everything, there is simply not room for a trinket, an objet d'art, a piece of jewelry, an ornament, a toy, a guilty pleasure, a piece of junk, or a collectible that is not a memory. Everything that sits on my shelves as part of one of my collections speaks to me in a way that sometimes only I can hear. They are remembrances of times that were good, friends that were near, and memories that were being made.

SANIA PELL

THE ROOM

The Room: when you stand in the doorway and look into your very own "room" it should take your breath away, make you feel calm and secure as if you are returning home, inspire you to create whatever is your passion of the day. This is your place and your time. This is your dream … and it should be exactly as you always believed that it could be.

If you are just beginning to plan your studio or you want to redesign your creative space, stand in the door one more time, close your eyes and imagine what you see. Sit at your desk or drawing table, locate your tools and supplies, open the drawers and the closet door. Now remember what color it is, where everything is placed, and what the furniture is made from. Write it down, draw your studio design on paper, recreate it from pages torn from magazines.

This is the time to begin and this is the place to be. This was once your dream that is soon to become your reality.

Large open spaces can be divided into smaller, more intimate working areas with the use of large windows or doors that are hung from the ceiling on each side of the room. This allows the expanse of well-organized space to be seen from any area of the office, yet creates separate, somewhat private spaces for each individual who works in or visits the studio.

Painting the studio one solid color makes the space appear even larger, and gives a sense of stability and uniformity. Who would not want to stand in the doorway of this studio and imagine all that could be created here!

Equally as inspirational and inspiring is the studio/office that is created in the spare bedroom. This is home; this is where your family can find you doing what it is you love to do best. The advantages of a small room are many: you can redesign and redecorate on a whim, you can move furniture from any room in the house into here without a shopping trip or a moving company, your kids can sit and play with you here or you can close the door for a private moment and know they are still part of your creative day.

When a studio space needs to be shared by two people this is a solution that is resourceful, original, and productive.

Two simple tables, two inexpensive chairs, memory boards that are understated—identical in that they both hold photographs, different in the memories that are recalled by the person whose photographs these are—and the shelves with the boxes … what is not to love about these shelves with these repetitive rows of boxes? It is stunning and calming, yet so stylish that it sets your mind reeling in a dozen different directions, each filled with different possibilities.

LAURA RESEN

This is a room in which you could work productively and allows you to leave home ... without actually going any place at all!

Organization is the art of creating a beautiful landscape. I love to work in a calm and beautiful environment with all of the things I love around me. An aesthetically pleasing landscape that's clean and organized is just the inspiration I need to create art.

The art of organization lies in having exactly what you need where you need it— and remembering where it is. If I can't see it, I often forget it's there. Antique glass display cases and glass door cupboards display my trinkets and fabrics and become art themselves, as well as organized storage. I strive to make everything within my view into a landscape that is efficient as well as visually pleasing.

-Nicol Sayre

NICOL SAYRE

Color. For me it's always about color. It creates order in the most diverse accumulation of objects. It ties together the most dissimilar of shapes.

When I style a room that's a jumble, I pick that most prominent color and add more of it. I subtract any other bright, distracting colors. The room becomes calm ... organized ... it flows.

The other day my neighbor asked for my help with her wall of shelving with its scattered objects and books. We began with white, then yellow, then orange, then red, grouping her books and objets d'art by color. And voila! The wall became a symphony!

—Sunday Hendrickson

As a visual designer, it's crucial for me to be able to see what I have, from the smallest bit and jewel, to millinery flowers and vintage wool blankets. Utilizing things like glass jars, glass front drawers, open shelving, and even old bottle racks, works great to not only show off my treasures, but to keep them at my fingertips.

Tools and supplies are still nearby, organized by function, in labeled drawers and boxes. Instead of keeping every bit of fabric, button and ribbon, I have learned to edit. Now, I keep only what inspires me, and sell or donate the rest. The best part of editing is that what is left defines me and my style, which does wonders for my creativity.
                                    -Michelle Jorgensen

1. CLEAN: Begin with a clean slate—I find it best to start from scratch. Clean, edit, and toss anything you don't need or want in your space.

2. UNIFORMITY: I think everything looks better in monochromatic form as far as organizing a space. Especially when boxes, files or binders hold a multitude of items, it is helpful to have them in a uniform container and labeled nicely. TIP: I use www.rebinder.com (plain recycled folders, binders, and cd cases).

3. LABELING/ PRETTY PENMANSHIP: For me, having everything nicely printed is an absolute MUST! TIP: If you aren't crazy about your handwriting, print out labels for a clean/ uniform look.

4. BEAUTIFY: Keep useful items and pretty collectibles where you can use and enjoy them. Add those extra special elements to your workspace to make it your own. TIP: Grandma's pitcher to hold flowers, vintage wrap to line drawers, etc.

5. CLUTTER FREE/ INSPIRATION: Keeping your space clean and organized and free of clutter leaves room for the things that inspire. I love to fill my work space with fresh flowers, special photographs, & quotes that remind me of what is most important.

-Kristin Alber

Not every creative space should be designed like an art room, or an office, or a guest bedroom that does double duty. Some should be fashioned after a kitchen. It is ingenious, really, and it's the heart of the home. Think about it: you would have all of the cupboard space you needed, a sink and dishwasher for your messier techniques and for cleaning up, a stove for the melting of wax, the mixing of dyes, or just making lunch without having to leave.

The kitchen is the perfect art room and, after all, it is from the kitchen table that we all began this creative journey we are on!

JESSIE WALKER

Not many of us will ever have a studio as elegant and sophisticated as this one—nor will we ever really need one—but it had to be included in this book on creative spaces because it is such a magnificent space filled with real light, rich hand-rubbed woods, and bottles of rare scents to make perfumes and lotions. Just the idea of sitting in this chair is a rare experience indeed!

DJ FREED

SUZAN STODDARD

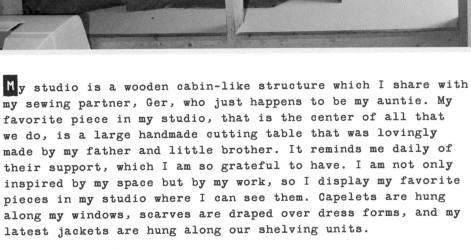

My studio is a wooden cabin-like structure which I share with my sewing partner, Ger, who just happens to be my auntie. My favorite piece in my studio, that is the center of all that we do, is a large handmade cutting table that was lovingly made by my father and little brother. It reminds me daily of their support, which I am so grateful to have. I am not only inspired by my space but by my work, so I display my favorite pieces in my studio where I can see them. Capelets are hung along my windows, scarves are draped over dress forms, and my latest jackets are hung along our shelving units.

I am drawn to a color palette made up of antique cream, smoky gray, and jet black. I love monochromatic color schemes. I like to think that this palette creates drama, vintage romance, and of course a little bit of haunted romanticism. Because color is so important to me I store my supplies and materials according to color, which enables me to find everything that I need for a project right away. All of the lace is in its own basket sectioned into color schemes, as is the case with the tulle, the beading fabric, and so on.

To continue with my philosophy of organization, when a project is near-finished, I like to keep it and all related parts in one open basket. Keeping everything related to that particular piece together makes it easy to come back to at a later time, when you are ready to finish it.

Clear jars are must-have storage units for me. I use them to store fabrics and ribbons according to color. For tools and materials that I don't readily need, I use containers according to size.

To be honest, I spend an unhealthy amount of time in my studio but I am blessed to work with Ger and together we create our own clothing with a distinctive romantic vintage vibe that is marketed under our own independent Irish design label.

                                        -Bonzie

Walls & Memory Boards

I am certain that the walls and the memory boards are the most revealing "picture" into anyone's creative genius. It is here you see what inspires them, what motivates them, what their dreams look like in print. Some are as complicated and as filled with ideas as the artists themselves. Some are simpler, monochromatic, more sensitive and introspective, again like the artist who created them.

These are the pages of the book of their creative life and if you look closely and pay attention, there is much here to learn and to share.

LAURIE LENFESTEY

SANIA PELL

SANIA PELL

CAROLINE TYLER DECESARE

CLASSIC & CLEAN

TIMELESS

LIGHT

BRIGHT

TAILORED

WHITE

NEUTRAL

Above my desk I have a simple piece of linen draped to the wall using five nails with ribbons wrapped around the nails to conceal them. It's a quick way to quickly collect your inspirations if you don't have time to run out and buy a giant pinboard.

I use washi tape and thumbtacks to keep all of my inspirations on the linen. Anyone can do it - it's so affordable and easy!

This IKEA cabinet may be meant for shoes but I use it for all of my office supplies - the drawers vary in size so it's perfect for storing all of my little collections, from business cards to postage stamps and ribbons.

If you cannot find your supplies easily, you'll become frustrated and drain your creativity. The better you organize your space, the more likely you will be to use the things you love to create!

-Holly Becker

HOLLY BECKER

LESLIE SHEWRING

It seems like organizing is part of my creative process. When I am organized I think clearer, my creating comes easier, and I find my supplies inspiring. Of course it all works the other way as well. When my studio is upside down, I feel the same way! I use the act of organizing my studio as a way to get out of my creative ruts. I am always amazed at the new stream of ideas I start having by simply going through my props and supplies with love, and giving them a new ordered place.

-Leslie Shewring

leslie shewring
ACREATIVEMINT.TYPEPAD.COM
LESLIESHEWRING.COM
ACREATIVEMINT@ME.COM

Poivre   Thé   C

LESLIE SHEWRING

Parrott Design Studio

zarah@parrottdesignstudio.com
www.parrottdesignstudio.com

leslie shewring

LINDA DURBANO

ARCKREALITY

MARCIA CEPPOS

LIFE'S TOUGH
GET A HELMET

LOVE FOR SALE

LEIGH STANDLEY

AVRIL JOFFE & CINDY JOFFE

DJ FREED

REBECCA PUIG

MONICA ADDISON

LAURIE LENFESTEY

GAIL RIEKE

JACKIE MATHEWS

Desks

Desktops are a mirror into an artist's soul. Is she complicated? Is she forever searching for yet another idea? Does she surround herself with anything and everything that she might need in her creative pursuit? What does the top of her desk tell you about her?

What I think I know is this: that the more creative she is, the less empty workspace you will see on her desktop. There are simply too many new ideas that need to be remembered and attempted to leave a space where nothing of importance is placed there.

GERI FROOMER

MONICA ADDISON

REBECCA PUIG

I am an artist and not organized by nature, but having cute containers around you really helps to inspire the Type A personality hiding within us all! I love to go to flea markets to find old wooden containers and metal bins and anything I can repurpose in a fun way! These old items really add a lot of soul to a space and make organizing way more fun. I put my paints in an old vintage box with stenciled numbers (which is an easy DIY project!)

also store things that I don't use on a daily basis in a big metal armoire so it doesn't clutter the space visually and mentally. Another trick is to make or buy an oversized corkboard to put photos, notes, or anything else you can imagine. I like to use old sewing pins or wooden pins instead of the plastic ones you see everywhere—I love little details like that. Lastly, I love to use sentimental items to organize with—I took an old jar from my grandmother's kitchen to use for my paintbrushes so it reminds me of her every time I paint!

-Rebecca Puig

REBECCA PUIG

REBECCA PUIG

DJ FREED

THE CABINET

The Cabinet: these are those spectacular pieces of furniture in our studios that demand our undivided attention. They are pieces of art that are useful and essential in their function of keeping us organized. We can salvage and give new life to discarded pieces or we can purchase a much-coveted piece that was somehow made just for our creative space and us. They can be big or small, tall or short, specific or redirected in their use ... what once was a wealthy woman's wardrobe can now hold papers and paints for an artist in the making.

Whatever they are, wherever we put them, we cannot live without them!

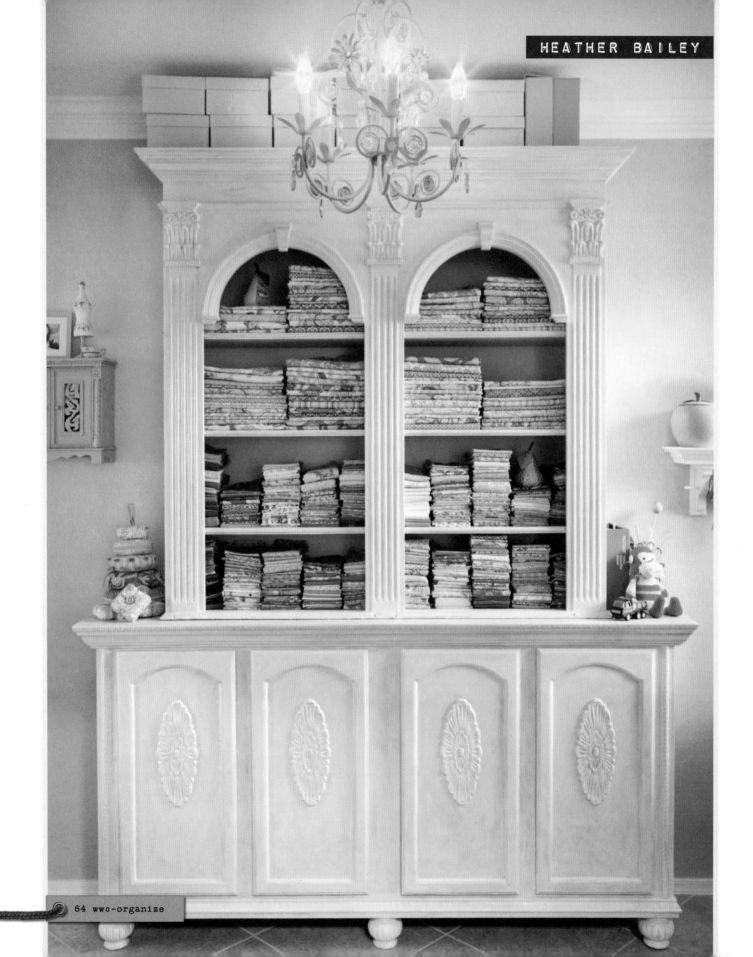

Candy Moger is a genius who creates fabulous pieces of "art" with fabric and furniture. She doesn't sell her work; she does what she does only for her own inspiration, luxury, and feelings of accomplishment. She has covered each of these pieces in her sewing room with her much loved yardage of vintage fabric. I envy her sitting in this room sewing, or reading, or wondering why everyone doesn't create their own space they love as much as she loves hers.

It's often all about the number of drawers in a cabinet ... the more it has the more you love it! I have to be very careful when I buy cabinets because I have to make certain that the drawers will actually hold the collected supplies and tools that I need a home for. I have purchased several pieces that had to be resold because the drawers were too small for me to actually use. And for me, everything must be filled and have a purpose.

DJ FREED

I covet long flat skinny drawers. They hold my papers that are so valuable to me that I am constantly worried about their edges being folded, tears down the side, or fingerprints appearing in the middle of their pages. In these drawers I am certain they are well protected from inquiring minds!

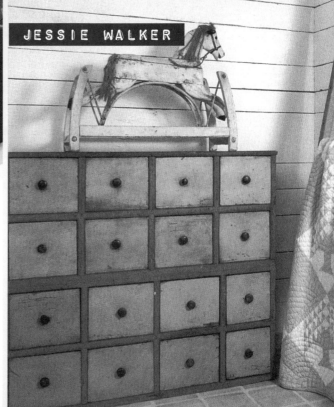

Vintage cabinets are my obsession of choice. I love their history, their patina, their quirky sizes, and their doors that don't quite fit or drawers that won't always close. These are pieces that have lasted through generations of families, that have held their wardrobes and displayed their wares that were for sale. These are pieces that come with a history and a story.

SUZAN STODDARD

SUZAN STODDARD

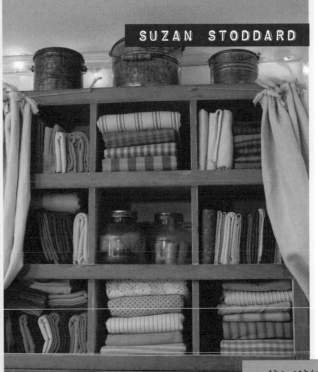
SUZAN STODDARD

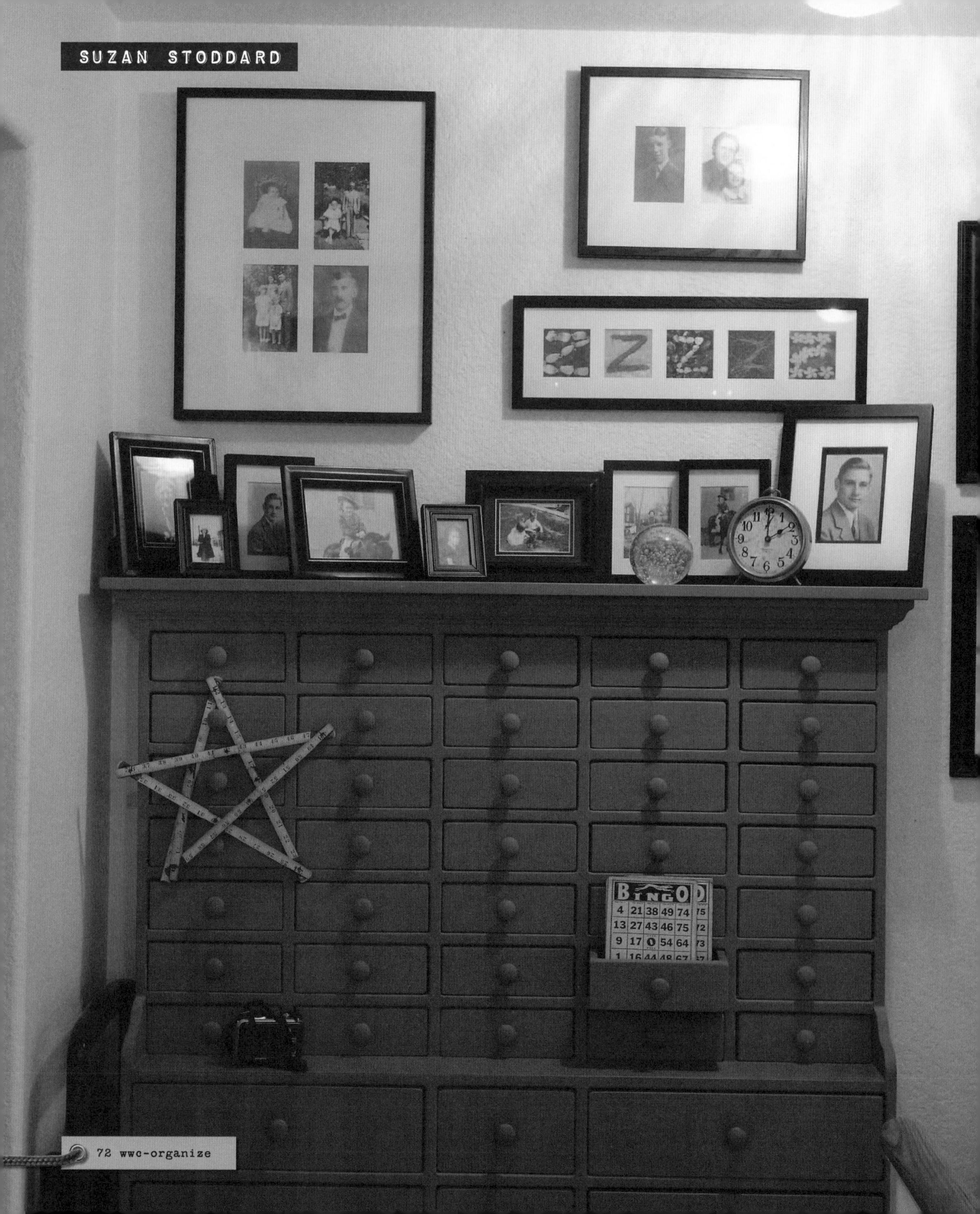
BINGO
4 21 38 49 74
13 27 43 46 75
9 17 O 54 64

Organization is not an action that one dabbles in. It is a habit that must be acquired and then maintained. It is not difficult to be organized, tools and techniques are available to all, but first the individual must have the desire and dedication to live an orderly life. Once committed, it is a simple process to become organized. Most individuals get bogged down at the start, frustrated at the overwhelming mess they have created. To offset the trepidation, work slowly and consistently until completion, and then dedicate a small portion of each day toward the goal of "everything in its place." Keeping to the ritual is key, and ensures it never again becomes the unscalable monolith of stuff.

-Suzan Stoddard

JESSIE WALKER

Drawers

For me there is nothing more spectacular or enviable than a room with high ceilings and cabinetry that requires a ladder to reach the uppermost shelves. These displays of grandeur are a statement of good taste, unquestionable quality, and skill of the finest craftsmen. This would be my dream ... floor to ceiling mahogany bookshelves filled with antique volumes of books, and matching adjoining cabinets overflowing with ribbons, lace, and rare papers.

WENDY ADDISON

WENDY ADDISON

METAL SHIMS
SLUGS
METAL BLOCKS
WOOD SPACERS
Antique Serif Type

WENDY ADDISON

I was famous as a child for being MESSY and DISORGANIZED! As an adult, I have made peace with what is my own internal system of organizing. Every object in my home and studio has some type of personal meaning and that is what guides me in figuring out how to store and use it. Thus, my antique paper collection is organized based on the memory of when and where I got it as in, this lot I found at the Alameda flea market, that lot from that guy who found his stuff in Quebec. In that sense, everything is organized according to memories of experiences.

I am one of those people who can work in a complete disaster zone and yet, reach over in a second and pull out that antique postcard I bought in 1978. I am like an ant who can re-trace each trace of where I have been, and recover any morsel. Most people who see me in my work mode are awed by the level of chaos I create around me, but I am most comfortable with it. I certainly do clean and organize on a regular basis, but only in preparation for making another creative mess! When things get clean and stay that way for too long, I get worried!

-Wendy Addison

SUZE WEINBERG

MANDY AFTEL

O rdinary drawers are suddenly extraordinary with the addition of the "perfect" knob. Buy them, make them, but use them ... everywhere!

KAARI MENG

DJ FREED

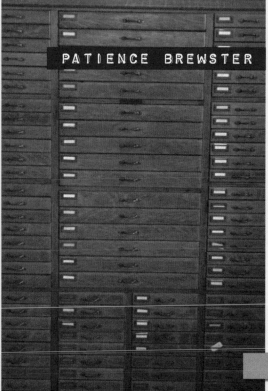

Life is too complicated not to be orderly. —Martha Stewart

GAIL RIEKE

GAIL RIEKE

GAIL RIEKE

SANIA PELL

I have a rule that I apply throughout my home and workspace: if I think something is beautiful and practical it can stay out on display. If it is not, then I relegate it to a storage box, drawer, or cupboard so it's out of sight. Surrounding myself with interesting items is inspiring and reminds me of the materials and tools I have to work with. Items like my vintage wooden and metal rulers and other old craft tools and implements such as vintage compasses, hefty metal scissors, and wooden set squares, that are full of character and are practical as well as beautiful. I keep these on display in front of my work desk; they give me joy to look at and are used on a daily basis.

I always buy vintage wooden crates and boxes of different sizes from flea markets and car boot sales (I think you call them garage sales or swap meets in the US), as they look great but hide whatever is inside with the lid down. Wooden box files are painted white and stamped with rubber alphabetical stamps for easy reference, but hide the messy jumble of papers, catalogs, and magazines behind them. Fabrics are kept clean in linen boxes stacked up on top of each other, though this system is rather more beautiful than practical as I can't tell what is inside the box until I have rifled through it! Embroidery threads are separated by color palette and stored in small clear, perspex drawer units. These are a pleasure to look at and easy to spot the required shade. Vintage cotton reels are kept out in little styled displays to be used and also to inspire. Canvasses and frames are stacked neatly in piles I find a pleasure to look at.

All of my small items, like inks, paints, brushes, and glues, I keep in a Boby trolley - a classic design from the 1970s by Joe Colombo - that has lots of drawers and compartments and is easy to wheel out when I work and then push away behind a door when I am finished.

-Sania Pell

PLAY &
WORK
& PLAY

KRISTIN ALBER

THE SHELF

The Shelf: they can be organized in as many ways as there are readers/artisans/organizers. And the "experts" each have their own favorite system that they are convinced you should adopt. However, my advice is that you do what is best for you and that is something that you usually just simply know instinctually.

The four options for organization on a shelf that I most prefer in order of preference are: by color, by subject/category, alphabetically, and by size … or a combination of any of these.

Color is by far and away the most beautiful, but the most difficult for me in ease of use. I will never be able to remember what color cover my favorite jewelry book has or what color box I put all of my sealing wax in.

By subject/category is the easiest for me, but when sitting in my office I am not inspired by that which surrounds me … and that, for me, is a bigger problem than not knowing what color the cover is. But with this method I always know where the paper supplies and books are in comparison to where the sewing threads and buttons are.

Alphabetically is another challenge for me, especially when it comes to names, because I cannot remember any author's name or any book's title. I can, however, remember that jewelry comes before scrapbooking in anyone's dictionary!

And size is used as a subhead with each of the above. Tallest on the left, shortest on the right, biggest on the bottom, smallest on the top or in the middle.

ANTIQUES

CAROLINE TYLER DECESARE

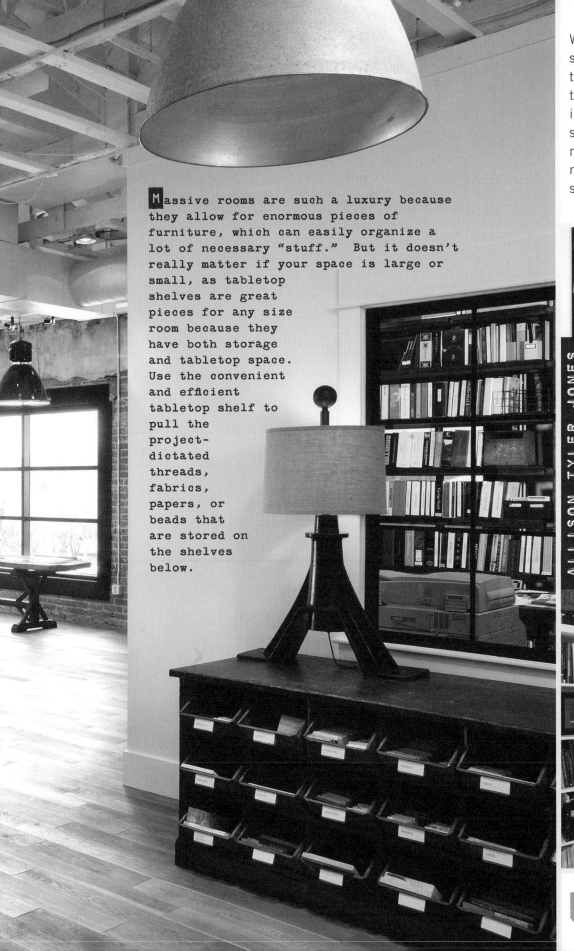

When looking for shelves, think beyond the "shelf"! You can turn almost anything into a functional funky shelving unit. The more unusual, the more inspired your surroundings.

Massive rooms are such a luxury because they allow for enormous pieces of furniture, which can easily organize a lot of necessary "stuff." But it doesn't really matter if your space is large or small, as tabletop shelves are great pieces for any size room because they have both storage and tabletop space. Use the convenient and efficient tabletop shelf to pull the project-dictated threads, fabrics, papers, or beads that are stored on the shelves below.

ALLISON TYLER JONES

MARYJANE BUTTERS

Let's say I want to take up the art of scrapbooking. Would it be a mistake to begin by tossing photos and trinkets into boxes under my bed? We all know the answer to that. The best bookkeeper I've ever employed shared this secret: handle a piece of paper only once. For example, when I open my mail, it goes to its proper place, not a "someday" box. Well, our creative lives are no different. If I don't keep my ideas sorted into lists of things-to-do, they overwhelm me. I turn them into long-term, short-term, and TODAY! lists (with lots of hearts scribbled in the margins).

-MaryJane Butters

SARAH CHAMPIER

I have two points of view that I am equally as passionate about but that are diametrically opposed to one another.

The first is that you can make something useful, functional, and fabulous from absolutely nothing, so save your money for purchases that you cannot make, such as vintage beaded fabric, rare old documents, or illustrated books that have long since become collectible.

The second is to save your money a little at a time for as long as it takes and buy one or two pieces of furniture that are useful, functional, and fabulous. It doesn't matter how expensive they are really, because they will be the "center" of your creative space and a constant source of inspiration and motivation.

Here Sarah Champier has created a series of shelf-like storage boxes from old crates. They are, indeed, useful, functional, and fabulous. On page 104 you will see a similar series of shelf-like metal storage boxes whose price tag is considerable but which I covet equally as much as Sarah's.

My recommendation: you must have both!

ANNE QUANTRANO

KRISTIN ALBER

Retail display trick: take multiple coffee tables, stack, create fabulous shelves!

KRISTIN ALBER

Whether your creative space is at home, in an old barn, or in the garage, hang up anything that inspires you.

KAARI MENG

TIM HOLTZ

Creating Color

What does one say about the power, the imagination, the inspiration of color? From my perspective, it is probably the most persuasive and pervasive component of how passionate we are about our studio ... whether we are working in it or someplace else just thinking about it.

There are hundreds of thousands of studies done and words written on the power of color and they are each an interesting read. My very simplistic recommendation for you and your creative space and color is to choose color—singular or multiple—that is all about you. Do not paint your walls or your furniture to match the rest of the house; do not choose a color that is more practical or more saleable, should you decide to do so; do not pick a color because it is #1 in the color trend forecast or because of an opinion or recommendation offered by your husband, your children, or a designer friend. Here, more than anywhere else, you absolutely must make the choice that is perfect for you!

I think all hunters and gatherers love to organize. I have always loved to organize by color. My love of organizing began at a very early age when I started to collect beads. I would sort all of the beads by color and then by size and then by material. I stored all of the vintage beads in old apothecary and jam jars. When I began designing jewelry with all of my beads, I found it so useful to be able to see everything at the same time- to have everything displayed in glass jars allowed me to come up with color palettes that I might never had thought of, if I was only designing on paper.

Even now, at French General, everything is displayed front and center—and always organized by color so that you can create an inspired story using ribbon, fabric or beads. Everything starts with color first.
                                                    -Kaari Meng

KAARI MENG

KAARI MENG

What works for me may not work for you. And what works for me right now may not work for me next month or next year. It's important to be flexible with your organization, always assessing and re-assessing what makes the most sense at the time, for your particular needs. If you work best with lots of stuff around you, put your most-used items in front of you, on your desktop, and in open shelves. If you need things to be clean and tidy to create your best work, keep the desktop clear and put things behind closed cupboard drawers as much as possible. I do think, in most cases, that it's a good idea to keep everything with its kind: all your writing instruments in the same drawer, all your paint in the same bin, all of your sketches, notes, and ideas in one notebook.

-Becky Higgins

There are certain things that will force even the most disorganized parts of us to get organized in a hurry. There is nothing quite as effective as a deadline.

I giggle a little when I use the word philosophy at all, mostly because I am not sure that given five words or less to describe me, anyone that knows me would use the word 'organized'. But I am. I have to be at a certain level. As a working creative I have deadlines and those deadlines require me to be able to get into my studio and make stuff as efficiently and splendidly as possible. Hunting around for 'that thing I know I have somewhere' really saps creative energy and can be distracting.

For me it is all about arranging the chaos. I like a bit of an organized mess, and I like to be able to see everything. So, for me it is about open shelving, small containers, glass front cabinets, bins, boxes, and jars. I can still see what I have, it just doesn't overwhelm me when I walk in the room. Everything has a beautiful little place.
                                    -Leigh Standley

LEIGH STANDLEY

MICHELLE JORGENSEN

JO PACKHAM

JULIE COVE

RIBBON ribbon RIBBON

Color or no color … use it with reckless abandon!

CONNIE GEOVA STUART

BETH QUINN

the shelf 101

MARCIA CEPPOS

For over 50 years, Tinsel Trading was run by my grandfather, Arch Bergoffen.

He was a loveable eccentric, and preferred to keep his store in complete and unattractive disarray. The dusty windows were piled with crumbling boxes, and the store was lined with sagging metal shelving. There was absolutely no organization.

But when I took over, 30 years ago, I took a deep breath and dove in. Over time and with help from my devoted staff, I managed to establish order and also create a beautiful store. I do not know whether he is frowning or beaming down at me, but customers can now see our vintage ribbons, flowers, tinsel, and trim lining the walls up to the 18' ceilings, organized by color and style!

The merchandise is also arranged so that as you go back in the store, you go back in history, and you will find metal trims from the early 1900s. My store windows blossomed from storage to stop-in-your-tracks eye-catching delights.

I saved all of the original storage boxes and cabinets from the basement and after dusting them out, used them to display treasures. And as I have a life long fondness for anything with lots of drawers, I use old ribbon cabinets, as well as type cases and thread display units to display my goodies. With time and hard work we went from total chaos to a visual delight enjoyed by many.

-Marcia Ceppos

MARCIA CEPPOS

NORMA RAPKO

Norma Rapko

NORMA RAPKO

REBECCA PURCELL

LETTERS LETTERS

There is something so
essential and necessary
about a piece of
furniture that "speaks"
to your very essence
of creativity and
organization … and it
is a different piece of
furniture for each of
us. But we all have that
"one" that the minute
we see it, it inspires
us, that haunts us long
after we have left the
store, and that is
simply the one that we
let get away!

This piece of furniture
is each of those for me.

KRISTIN ALBER

Nook & Cubby

ANNE QUANTRANO

JESSIE WALKER

What is it, exactly, about the repetition of a single object that we find so fascinating, so inspiring, and so visual? Every time we see it, it is as if we are seeing it again for the first time.

DJ FREED

JO PACKHAM

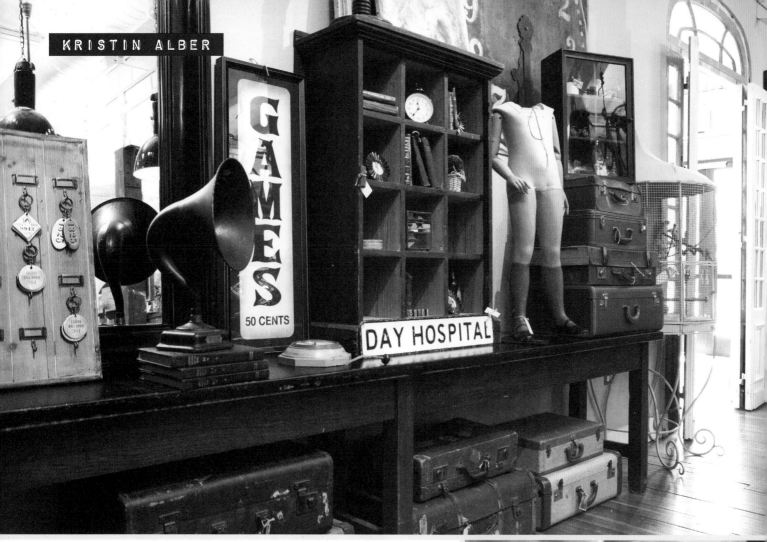

KRISTIN ALBER

GAMES

50 CENTS

DAY HOSPITAL

The perfect cubical is essential to hold, organize, and display "all" of our collections, supplies, tools, and finished handmade pieces. We each love them; we shop tirelessly for them; we buy lots of them; we are always looking for just one more that is a little different size, whose cubbies are a little bigger or a little smaller, whose exterior is more aged, a different color, or glass vs. wood. We simply can never have too many … or enough.

We use our imagination to turn something, anything, every thing into a cubical. The photo to the right is a wire wine rack … what took me so long to find it?!

ANNE QUANTRANO

What is most difficult about books such as this one, displays in our favorite design stores, or shopping at an out-of-town flea market is that we always see the much "dreamed of" furniture piece for our studio and we know in our heart we will never have the opportunity to actually own it! How can one piece of furniture cause frustration from not owning it and wanting to, satisfaction from knowing it does exist and that someone else is inspired by it daily, and optimism because someday we may just have the good fortune to bring one home that is exactly as we remember this one!

DJ FREED

Your creative space is by far the most influential aspect of inspiration. My best advice is to make the most of what you have, and most importantly do what works for you. I have a very random thought process when I'm creating and therefore prefer to have as many of my supplies out in the open as possible to see...rummage through...and best of all...get used. What works for me are metal shelving, wire baskets, and glass jars because they are readily available in all shapes and sizes and I can see their contents at a glance. I'm considered a digger I suppose, someone who prefers to dig through my stash instead of trying to remember what little drawer or container I tucked it away in. I think it inspires me when I am creating because I might come across something I wasn't even looking for in the first place.

Sure it's still important to have some sense of organized chaos, but bottom line, this works for me. I group my supplies by what they are really: ribbons, papers/tags, tools, adhesives, etc. so they are easy to locate, but again give me options of what I might use. Sturdy metal shelving cannot only support the weight, but are also completely customizable. I'm also a collector like most, so vintage wire baskets and glass jars are the perfect solution to fill with all of my treasured findings. This is not only functional, but also visually inspiring by simply having everything on display.

They say you can never have too much of a good thing, and when it comes to rubber stamps I completely agree. Of course the challenge of storage definitely comes to mind. In order to keep them all visible I start with standard bookcases and add a little creative altering. By using a strip of insulation foam found at the hardware store, I was able to create risers on each shelf. This provides a place for an additional row of stamps without adding excess weight to the shelf. I display my stamps at an angle to allow for more stamps in less space, but still show part of each image making it easy to find just the image I need...function and inspiration.

When it comes to organizing remember to make it inspiring, make the most of your space, and make it work for you. Finally supply meets solution...

-Tim Holtz

TIM HOLTZ

White Bright

And there is also something mesmerizing about painting an entire room the same color—walls, ceiling, woodwork, cubbies, and closets. What is it that draws us into a space like this? Does the repetition of color throughout the room afford a sense of security, stability, and predictable expectation? Is such an approach to design and color a step that is very, very safe or is it a daring statement of creative courage?

There is something sheerly magical in the use of color with no color. It is so easily created by some and so impossible to find just the right balance by others. I am one of those that loves the absence of color with a short bold statement of it that immediately captures your attention. I have tried time and time again to recreate the "essence of color design" on these two pages. I have finally come to the realization that it is going to have to be enough for me to enjoy such design on the pages of magazines and books and to envy those whose talent is so brilliant and bold!

SANIA PELL

SANIA PELL

CAROLINE TYLER DECESARE

Order is the shape upon which beauty depends. —Pearl S. Buck

CAROLINE TYLER DECESARE

HOLLY BECKER

CAROLINE TYLER DECESARE

The secret of all victory lies in the organization of the non-obvious. —Marcus Aurelius

LAURIE LENFESTEY

Many lessons for creative organization can be learned from those women who own, design, and manage their own retail establishments. One such lesson is the inexpensive, functional, easy-to-care-for, multiple-use shelving units that they must create for their stores.

These are the perfect models for studio use when product is produced for sale. A large shelving unit should be broken down and constructed in groups of smaller units so that the entire structure can be dismantled, moved, rearranged, or reconfigured easily.

The units should be painted with a high quality paint that does not scratch as easily as lower paint grades might. The primer coat when painting the shelves should be the same color as the topcoat. The color should be one that is universal so that it creates a stage for all items that are being stored or displayed there.

BETH QUINN

When putting the finished retail pieces on the shelves, put a piece of paper on the bottom of each shelf to protect the shelf from scratches. This can be paper that is the same color as the shelf so it is barley noticeable or papers that are different and become part of the display.

Organization of product is a challenge at best, especially when the product is stored and shipped from the studio. It is important that this aspect of studio production be as artfully organized as the rest of the studio, which will create several opportunities: the first is that with each new day of standing in front of these shelves beautifully displayed with your pieces, you will continually be inspired to create more and different product to add to your line. Second: you can use your studio as a retail outlet for occasional or studio sales, saving overhead in so many areas when your business and studio are new.

SALLY JEAN ALEXANDER

CAROLINE TYLER DECESARE

CAROLINE TYLER DECESARE

BRIGHT

When your creative area is limited and there is much to organize, the secret is to not waste any available space, regardless of where it is. Putting two identical cubical containers at each end under the table—and covering the sides of the table with a tablecloth—offers much needed, easily accessible, and lovely storage for important supplies, tools, or inventory.

SUZAN STODDARD

THE CONTAINER

The Container: it is an obsession with most creatives ... there are so many possibilities for the all of the "stuff" that we have for which we need interesting, yet functional, items to hold them. But it can't just be anything—it must be vintage or new, colored or clear, large or small. And the details are essential: any old lid will not suffice and the closure is as important as the container itself.

These are the items that fill our shelves, our desktops, and our drawers. They are pieces of art that hold those purchases most precious to our very existence as artists. We never have enough, we can never buy too many, we constantly change directions so there are always new glasses and jars and boxes that must be found and purchased without delay!

Metal

KRISTIN ALBER

KRISTIN ALBER

FOUND

KRISTIN ALBER

PILLOWTALK

CAROLINE TYLER DECESARE

When shopping your local flea market or garage sale think about "all" that everything you see can be used for once you get it home. Metal industrial bins can hold bolts of fabric, vintage shopping carts can hold single projects that need to be transported, and mail baskets can be hung on the wall filled with fat quarters or paper work. Not everything need be square and sit on a shelf!

KAARI MENG

JOANNA FIGUEROA

JOANNA FIGUEROA

JOANNA FIGUEROA

TIM HOLTZ

TIM HOLTZ

TIM HOLTZ

SUNDAY HENDRICKSON

SUZAN STODDARD

Metal crates and baskets are a favorite for all of us, but please clean them carefully; you might even consider spraying them with a clear coating to keep them from rusting. You want to protect those items that have been placed in these rare and wonderful finds for safekeeping.

BETH QUINN

REBECCA RAY

TIM HOLTZ

JO PACKHAM

MELODY ROSS

I have had to find ways to organize my large collection of supplies that works for me, which means that I know that I can, and will, put things back where they go easily, and that I can find things easily, and especially that I can see what I have...I truly enjoy looking at the beauty of my art stuff! I would say that my biggest organizational philosophy is happiness...if it's pretty and easy to keep up, it makes me so happy and doesn't feel like a chore to put things away.

What works for me is to organize my treasures by color. I love to look at everything in the order of a rainbow, and it makes it so easy to put things back where they go when I am done using them. It also makes it so easy to find what I am looking for, and it is exceptionally easy to feel inspired by the beauty of everything... when I have decided on a color scheme and I can just pull the paint, fabric, beads, and ephemera in those colors and just get to work.

I keep scraps of all kinds for collage. So you will find boxes of fabric scraps organized by color, boxes of paper scraps organized by color...and then all sorts of funny things that would work in mixed media art ... all organized by color. I love working this way!

I look for organizational containers that are easy to see into. A lot of my things are in glass or clear plastic, so that I can see what is in the container from a distance. Once everything is organized into color, it is put on the shelf in rainbow order. It is like its own work of art to see everything on the shelves this way. It makes me happy every time I look at it!

-Melody Ross

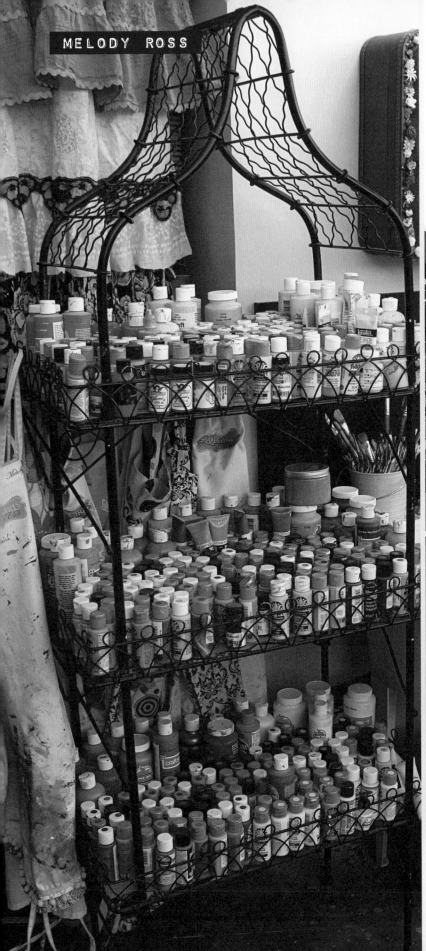

MELODY ROSS

MELODY ROSS

WENDY ADDISON

Glass

MICHELLE JORGENSEN

LESLIE SHEMRING

MARTHA YOUNG

CONNIE GEOVA STUART

Anything can be filled with something and, once it is, where are you going to put it and how is it going to be organized and categorized? You might want to answer these questions before you begin to fill your bottles and boxes. If you have decided to arrange your jars by solid color contents, then you want to be careful not to inadvertently fill some of them with multi-colored spools of threads or bags of marbles or a variety of plastic colorful toys.

TIM HOLTZ

KAARI MENG

MARTHA YOUNG

NORMA RAPKO

When you use bottles and jars without their lids for storage containers, make certain that you save the lids in a box and remember where it is. You are going to need them one day, that is a given!

Creating order in my studio is an ongoing process. As interests and projects evolve, so do my needs and approach to keeping everything organized and sorted.

As a very visual person I am happiest surrounded by those things that hold good memories and inspire my art. At the same time, I really do not thrive with a lot of clutter.

Fun and funky containers, industrial storage and timeworn antiques are my solution. Bring in that wooden tool box and make it you own. Pick up that mechanic's set of drawers for auto parts and organize your supplies.

-Jennifer Pearson Vanier

JENNIFER PEARSON VANIER

KRISTIN ALBER

MANDY AFTEL

Woven

SUZAN STODDARD

JESSIE WALKER

REBECCA PUIG

NICOL SAYRE

JOANNA FIGUEROA

JOANNA FIGUEROA

As with most creative types, I enjoy living in a world of colorful, creative chaos. I thrive on seeing all of my materials, colors, and each and every print as I work to see what story the colors will tell me. Without that kind of freedom to see, touch, and feel all of my fabrics, paints, or colored pencils, I couldn't work at all. Yet organization is a vital component of my creative process.

For me organization has to be open, accessible, and most of all, pleasing to look at. I love to use vintage cubbies, matching baskets, open wood shelving, and antique wire baskets with vintage labels. The form of the organization itself has to be beautiful and a part of my overall decor. My organized areas are a part of my daily living and can't be tucked away from sight. Instead I have to see everything in order to use it. So I organize it in plain sight.

-Joanna Figueroa

Mugs & Bowls

NICOL SAYRE

REBECCA PUIG

BETH QUINN

ANNE QUANTRANO

HEATHER BAILEY

LAURIE LENFESTEY

ALISA BARRY

When looking for containers in a variety of shapes and sizes to hold your trinkets and treasures, look in unexpected nontraditional places for them. Juice glasses in a kitchen store will work, as will small cereal bowls and even smaller milk cups. And a favorite of mine are the variety of small glass bowls in the "designer" section of discount stores. They are usually quite inexpensive and they are perfect for jewelry findings, small amounts of different colors of paint, office supplies that are needed during crafting, and all of our additional everyday essential supplies like brushes, scissors, pencils and pens.

And then take one step further while in the kitchen store or at your local flea market and carefully examine every item that can hold something. Condiment dishes are perfect for this, as are old silver sugar bowls and creamers, or small crystal dessert dishes that someone's great aunt could no longer find a use for.

SUNDAY HENDRICKSON

REBECCA RAY

TIM HOLTZ

JULIE WEISS

CONNIE GEOVA STUART

CONNIE GEOVA STUART

Suitcases are so romantic ... where have they been, what have they seen, what stories do they have to tell? When you use them for storing your fabrics, threads, laces, buttons and beads, or stacks of papers, unfilled albums, and boxes of pictures waiting to be pasted to their pages, they are easily organized, fabulous stacked on top of each other in your workroom, and a constant source of inspiration.

The inside of your suitcase is easily organized with the use of small boxes. Cigar boxes are often times the better choice because they are not too tall, you can stack them on top of one another inside the case, and they are as interesting as the suitcases themselves.

VICTORIA MACKENZIE-CHILDS

GAIL RIEKE

The studios are working spaces, installation environments, and gallery rooms. My husband and I have been collaborating on this project for about 25 years. The studios contain many drawers where many pieces are accessible while awaiting completion. The structure of the studio echoes my working process. One wall is a floor to ceiling structure which houses antique suitcases, boxes, baskets and trunks. Each container pulls out from the wall and opens to display a combination of drawings, photos, collages, textile works, books, and objects that often recall past travel. A formal continuity and structure unites the diverse media in each work.

-Gail Rieke

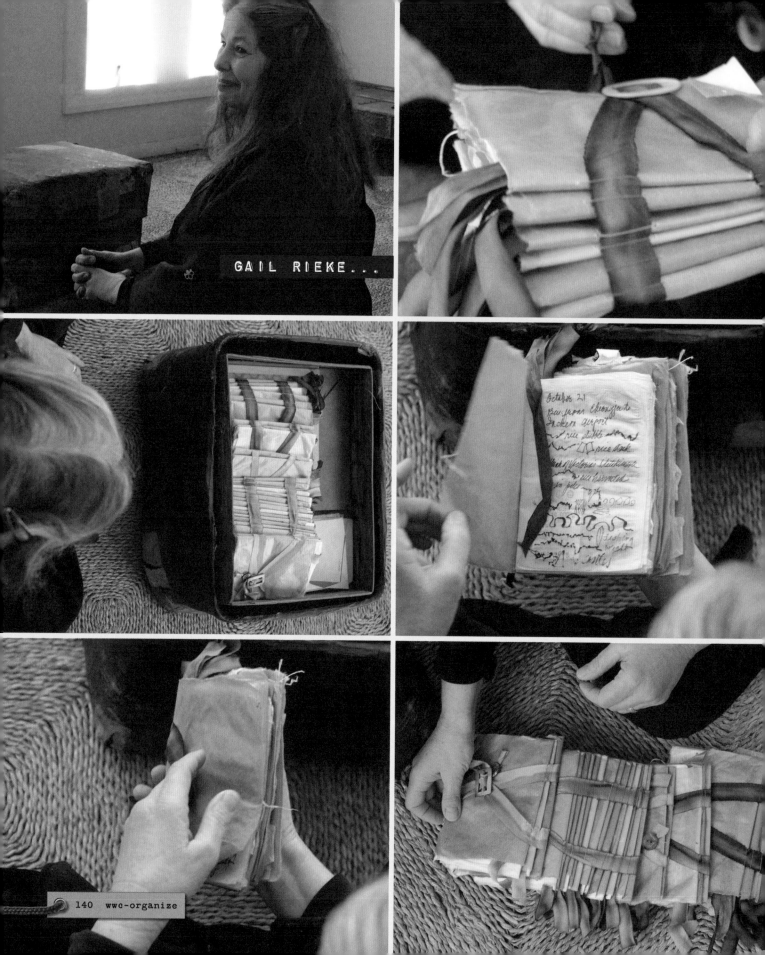

GAIL RIEKE...

When it comes to organizing my art supplies, the only thing I keep in mind is that I need to be able to see and get to everything easily. If items are put away in drawers or in boxes, I'll forget they're there. I need to be able to see what I have at a glance. When I create, I tend to get in a "zone" so it's important that everything is easily accessible, or else I'll use the same three supplies that are within reach. I think this suitcase project perfectly shows my organizing philosophy: everything is visible for me to grab without much thought.

-Christen Olivarez

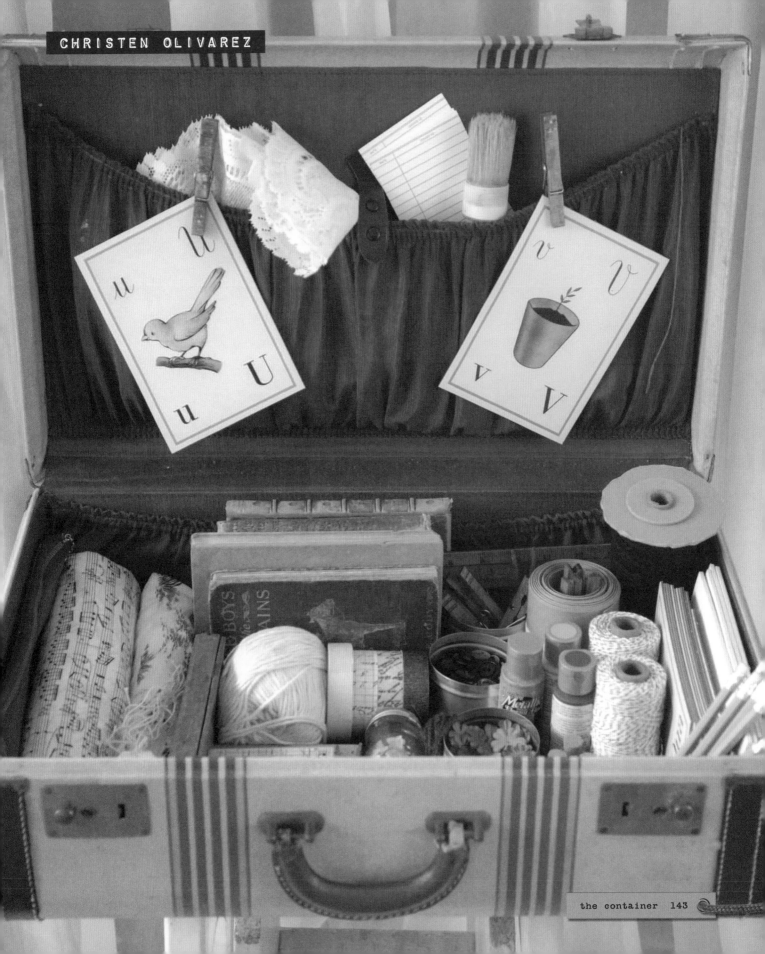

MICHELLE JORGENSEN

ANNE QUANTRANO

Crates

When selecting storage pieces to organize your larger spools of threads, your magazines, your skeins of yarn, your stacks of fat quarters, your scrapbooking papers, and a hundred other things, ask your local grocery stores, farmers market, and garden stores for their empty crates. Many times they will give them to you for free because they view them in much the same way that a shipper sees an empty, once-used box.

If the crates have been used for fresh food, wash them well in the sink, the shower, or with the garden hose, put them in the sun to dry thoroughly, and then leave them the color they are or, as with these grey crates, dye them with a wood stain or diluted paint. You can even stamp on them with your favorite rubber stamps or add exotic stickers and images cut from magazines that can be decoupaged on the sides.

DJ FREED

KRISTIN ALBER

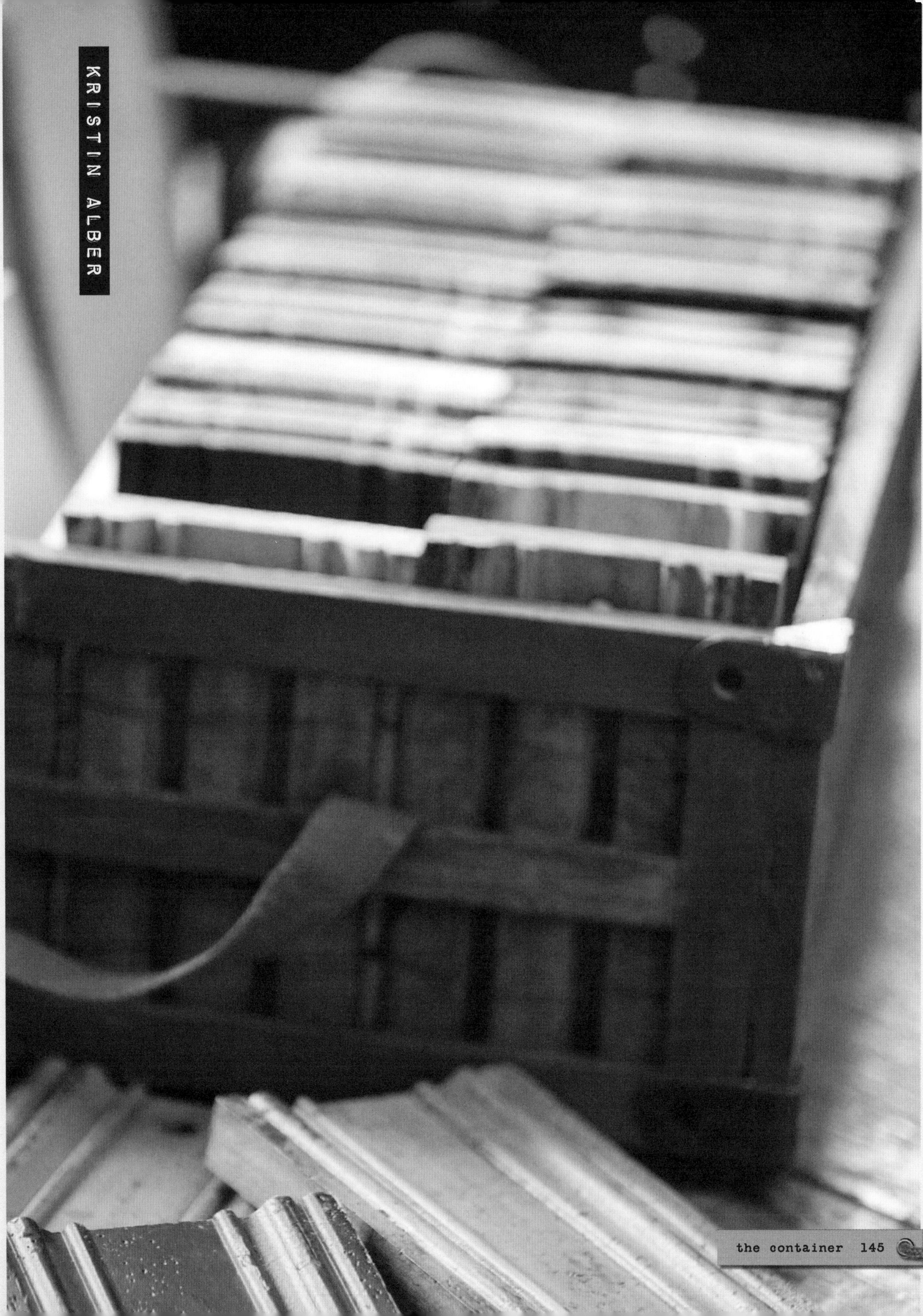

REBECCA PURCELL

Trays

When organizing smaller items, trays are both a source of fascination and a necessity. Buy the great ones that you find but also, remember: you can make some of your own.

WENDY ADDISON

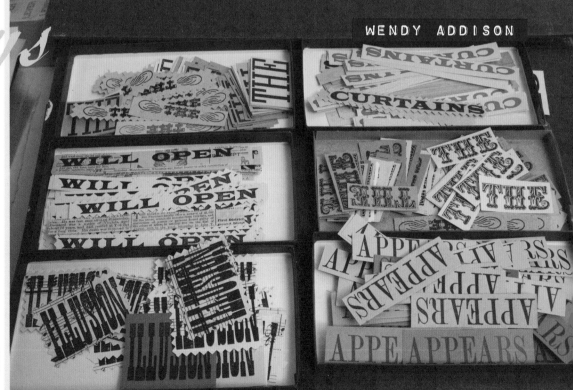

REBECCA PUIG

Organizing small items will lead you into a world of creating trays perfect to organize them. You can create your own tray by purchasing flat serving trays or using sturdy box tops and filling them with smaller boxes that are arranged like the pieces of a puzzle, each holding your smallest random treasures.

Jewelry supply houses have wonderful flat black boxes with glass tops that can be used for small paper items, beads and findings. Also, check your local vintage stores for trays that were used to store hardware or garden supplies—it is here you will find the printers' trays whose tiny compartments can be used for hundreds of small items that are often lost at the bottom of a bigger box or easily misplaced.

CONNIE GEOVA STUART

KAARI MENG

JACKIE MATHEMS

Being a visual person, I like to see everything ... seeing everything inspires me in every way—and yet, I don't like clutter so organizing my supplies can be tricky. It's a fine balancing act, trying to decipher how much to show and tell and how much to cloister away ... to inspire, not clutter.

I am free spirited by nature and love space and possibilities but systems hold my creativity in a safe way.

With that said, in my studio, there is a real system ... a place for everything so I know where to reach when the mood strikes. One key point is that it looks like there is no system. I like it to look and feel artistic, not like a business office, so the systems in and of themselves are creative—I found the most lovely vintage locker bins at a flea market in California-they are painted a gorgeous regal blue—and they are housed in an old hutch I found along the way of a wonderful trip. So the systems have feelings—and house and inspire happy memories.

A few years ago, while I was away on vacation, an assistant thought she would tidy up my workspace and get it organized ... wow! did that feel like a violation! I couldn't find a thing and every time I went to just reach for a certain brush, or pen or lens, it was nowhere to be found. My intuition could not guide me through "her system" ... I then needed to use my head, and once I am out of intuitive mode and have to be in my head, my creativity dwindles—fast.

So my advice is to trust yourself, to find your own systems so that you can sink into your creativity ... seeing your supplies to inspire you, but have beautiful folders, bins (I use wonderful vintage locker bins painted a beautiful blue) to house in the chaos so the creativity can unfold.

-Laurie Lenfestey

Organizers

MARTHA YOUNG

TIM HOLTZ

Organizers can be found on almost every shelf at your local Bed Bath & Beyond or The Container Store, and of course, IKEA. Look in the kitchen department where there are endless choices and designs of drawer and shelf organizers for kitchen utensils and supplies. They come in wood, plastic, and metal. And don't forget the bedroom department for hanging organizers that were designed for shoes but are also ideal for ribbons and other craft supplies.

MARTHA YOUNG

MARTHA YOUNG

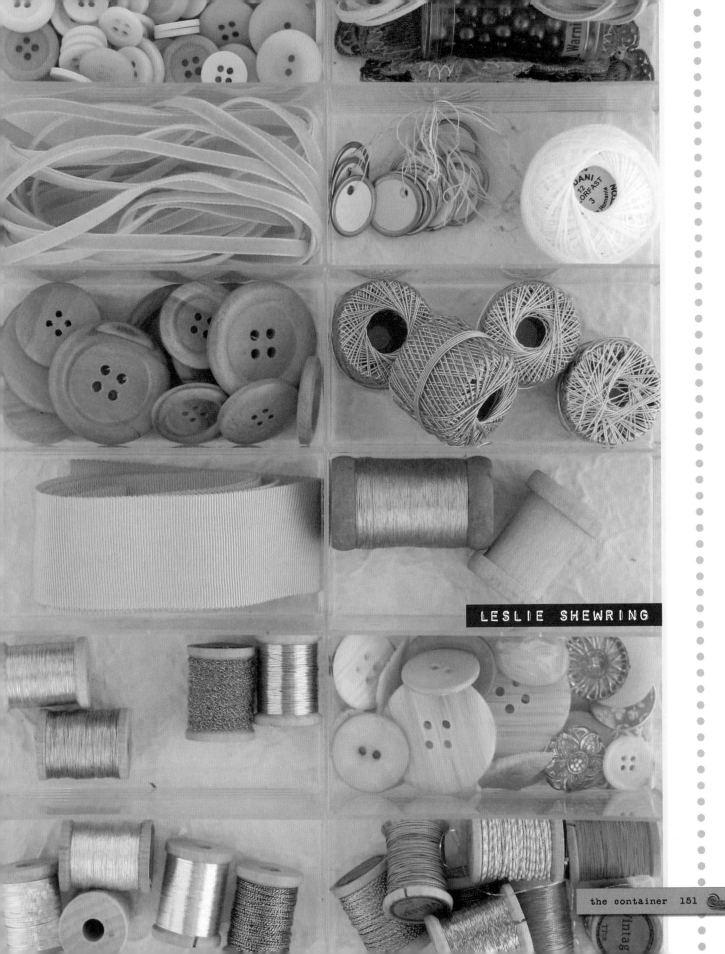

LESLIE SHEWRING

WENDY ADDISON

Boxes

JO PACKHAM

152 wwc-organize

NICOL SAYRE

Christmas

MICHELLE JORGENSEN

CLOTH   METAL

LEATHER
WOOD   FROG CLOSURES   RHINESTONE

LEIGH STANDLEY

ALISA BARRY

Bags

SANIA PELL

Using bags as units of organization was something that I had never thought of until I was on a photo shoot at Sania Pell's home in London. She had canvas bags that she had collected hanging on her studio door and in each was a different project that she could simply grab and take with her when she was traveling.

What a great idea this is, and after my introduction to an entirely new series of organizing possibilities I began to see options everywhere I looked.

JESSIE WALKER

KAARI MENG

KAARI MENG

SUZAN STODDARD

LEIGH STANDLEY

JUDY WATKINS

the Rest

I am fairly certain that we all have somewhat of an obsession with items that can be used for storing and organizing. I think I know this because everywhere we go we look for them and every one we see we buy. After all, if we don't need it today we will someday and when we return to purchase it, it might already be part of someone else's studio.

CAROLINE TYLER DECESARE

ANNE QUANTRANO

MARTHA YOUNG

BONZIE

ANNE QUANTRANO

TIM HOLTZ

ANNE QUANTRANO

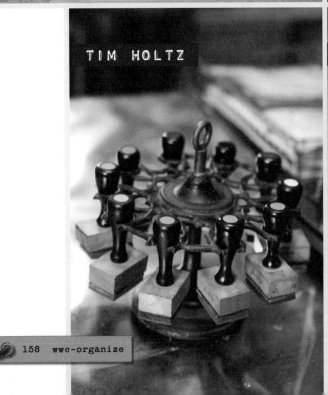

KAARI MENG

JOANNA FIGUEROA

THE COLLECTION

JO PACKHAM

The Collection: volumes have been written about, magazine dedicated to, and professional papers submitted on people and their collections. Collections are as varied as screwdrivers and diamond rings, as fascinating as vintage beaded bags and retro bakelite drawer handles They can be both expensive and free, big and little, necessary and a useless guilty pleasure ... but they are important to each of us in their own subjective and imaginative way.

Buy them for yourself, don't feel guilty about your purchase, organize and arrange them where they can be seen and appreciated. There is a reason that we are all collectors ... we don't need to understand it; we simply need to trust it.

AVRIL JOFFE & CINDY JOFFE

Wearables

We love to collect jewelry. Sometimes all kinds of jewelry, sometimes more specific designs, artists, or materials. It started when we were children playing in our mother's jewelry boxes and dressing up as if we too were going to the ball with such a handsome man.

I simply have to display my jewelry where it can be seen. If I don't, then I sometimes forget what I have, I misplace my favorite pieces, and if they are put away, then I am not allowed to enjoy the sheer beauty of each piece every single day. For me, something is not worth having if it cannot be seen, touched, and admired.

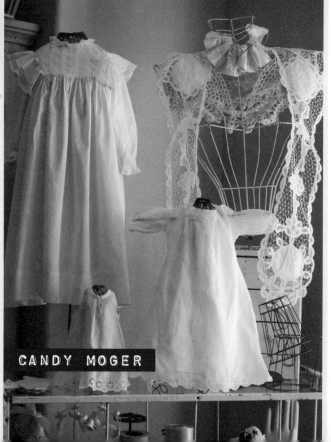

CANDY MOGER

DJ FREED

TIM HOLTZ

LAURIE LENFESTEY

SANIA PELL

CONNIE GEOVA STUART

LAURIE LENFESTEY

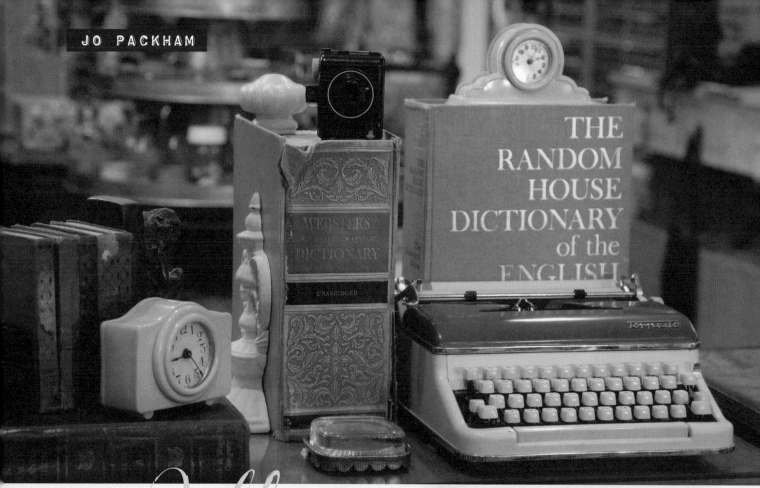

JO PACKHAM

...and More

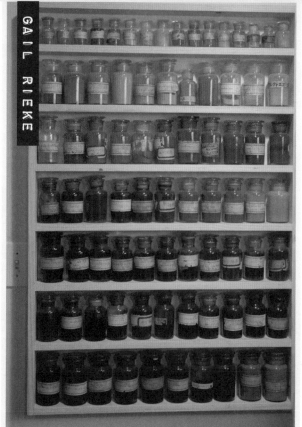

GAIL RIEKE

Collections are personal and should tell the story of what is important to you. Don't collect items because they were someone else's treasured pieces, because they may be "valuable" someday, or because now you have so many of something that they have unknowingly become a collection.

Collect that which is a window into who you are. This partial collection of books, a typewriter, a camera, and clocks is everything in one small place that is part of my everyday life. Books are who I am and what I do, time is something to be treasured because we never know how much of it we have, and the camera takes the pictures that is the art on the pages of my books. I love this collection of mine so it sits on the corner of my desk.

Collections are sometimes those items that you actually use. Don't be afraid to wear, utilize, and enjoy those pieces that you have collected. Display your dishtowels, but use them daily to dry the dishes. Wear your vintage pieces of clothing, as they are much sought after by the design houses of Europe. And take the game pieces off the wall and out of the drawers and spend your leisure hours with your children in much the same way as your grandmother once did.

JESSIE WALKER

MARTHA YOUNG

VICTORIA MACKENZIE-CHILDS

MANDY AFTEL

REBECCA PURCELL

GERI FROOMER

JESSIE WALKER

NICOL SAYRE

NICOL SAYRE

NICOL SAYRE

MONICA ADDISON

KAARI MENG

It is just confusing to buy decorative pieces of art for your home when you have wonderful collections that could be used in their place. Why go to your local department store and buy a print that has been reproduced thousands of times and hangs in hundreds of homes and offices, when you can hang your vintage wearables on the wall in your bedroom from a clothesline or a ribbon? It is your home and your "art" that will be the subject of conversation at neighborhood dinner parties ... why let them talk about somebody else?!

SUZAN STODDARD

THE INDEX

CONNIE GEOVA STUART

LESLIE SHEWRING

NICOL SAYRE

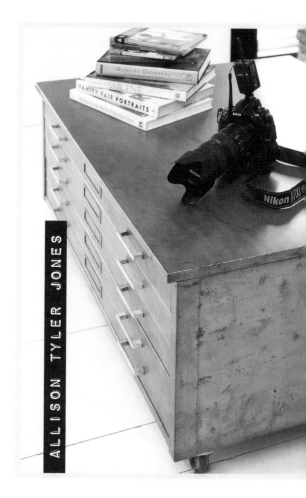

ALLISON TYLER JONES

CAROLINE TYLER DECESARE

NO... IT GOES HERE

WHAT'S A CONTAINER?

A PLACE FOR EVERYTHING...

AND EVERYTHING IN ITS PLACE

I AM ORGANIZED!